SCIENCE FILES

CHEMICALS & CHANGE

SCIENCE FILES – CHEMICALS AND CHANGE
was produced by

David West ⚥ Children's Books
7 Princeton Court
55 Felsham Road
London SW15 1AZ

Designer: Gary Jeffrey
Editor: Gail Bushnell
Picture Research: Carlotta Cooper

First published in Great Britain by Heinemann
Library, Halley Court, Jordan Hill, Oxford
OX2 8EJ, part of Harcourt Education.
Heinemann is a registered trademark
of Harcourt Education Ltd.

08 07 06 05
10 9 8 7 6 5 4 3 2 1

ISBN 0 431 14319 6 (HB)
ISBN 0 431 14326 9 (PB)

British Library Cataloguing in Publication Data

Parker, Steve
Chemical changes. - (Science files)
1. Chemical reactions - Juvenile literature
I. Title
541.3'9

Printed and bound in China

PHOTO CREDITS :
Abbreviations: t-top, m-middle, b-bottom, r-right,
l-left, c-centre.

Front cover - bl & br - Digital Stock. Pages 3 &
14bl, 18 both - Corbis Images. 4–5 & 12–13, 6–7,
10t, 11r, 12t, 16l, 17, 22r, 23 both - Digital Stock.
8t - NASA. 13 - M. Watson/ Ardea London Ltd.
21, 22l, 22–23, 24 - Rex Features Ltd. 27b -
Castrol. 29l - Katz Pictures.

Every effort has been made to contact copyright
holders of any material reproduced in this book.
Any omissions will be rectified in subsequent
printings if notice is given to the publishers.

With special thanks to the models: Felix Blom,
Tucker Bryant and Margaux Monfared. Also to
Bemrose Dry Cleaners.

*An explanation of difficult words can be
found in the glossary on page 31.*

SCIENCE FILES

CHEMICALS & CHANGE

Steve Parker

Heinemann LIBRARY

CONTENTS

WARNING! All projects should be supervised by a responsible adult. Some need extra care and expert help, and are marked with a red box. Make sure the instructions are followed. *Never take risks.*

INTRODUCTION

All around us are objects and materials, from tables and chairs to brick walls, cars, trees, clouds in the sky and invisible gases in air. They are all made of chemical substances, and many are produced by altering other chemical substances. The science of chemicals and how they change is vital in today's world, and in tomorrow's world.

How it WORKS

These panels explain the science behind the projects, and the processes and principles that we see every day, but which we may not always understand!

PROJECT PANEL

The projects are simple to do with supervision, using household items. Remember – scientists are cautious. They prepare equipment thoroughly, they know what should happen, and they *always* put safety first.

ELEMENTS AND ATOMS

It may seem that there is an endless number of materials and substances around us. Different kinds of woods, soil, metals, glass, textiles, rocks – the list is huge. Science shows that it's not so complicated.

Most elements are spread out through Earth's rocks. They can be obtained in pure form by various processes, such as melting the rock in a furnace, as here with the metal nickel.

SMALLEST PARTS

Imagine trying to divide a substance into smaller and smaller parts, using chemical processes. Finally the particles would be so tiny, you could not split them further. The smallest particles of a substance are atoms. There are less than 100 different natural kinds of atoms. A substance made of only one kind of atom is a chemical element. These are shown in the chart.

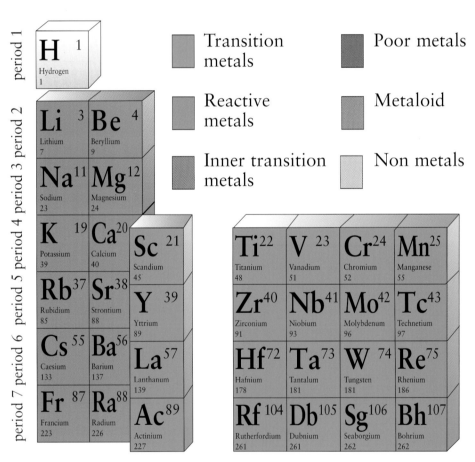

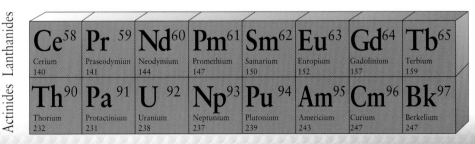

An atom has a central nucleus of protons and neutrons, orbited by electrons.

ATOMS AND ELEMENTS

All the materials, objects and substances around us are a combination of billions and billions of atoms. Some atoms are very common in many different substances, others are incredibly rare.

How it WORKS

All elements are shown in the periodic table. Rows of the table are called periods. Elements in a period become less ready to join or react with others from left to right. Columns of the table are called groups. Elements in a group share chemical features, but they get heavier from top to bottom. About 88 elements occur naturally. The rest are made using scientific equipment like 'atom-smashers'.

Chemical formula or symbol

Atomic number (number of protons)

Name of element

Atomic mass (relative 'weight')

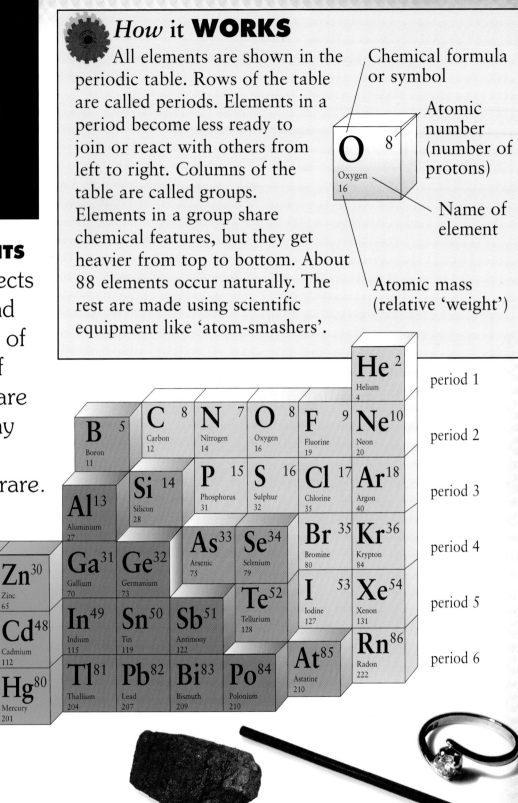

O	8	
Oxygen 16		

He 2 — Helium 4 — period 1

B 5 Boron 11 | C 8 Carbon 12 | N 7 Nitrogen 14 | O 8 Oxygen 16 | F 9 Fluorine 19 | Ne 10 Neon 20 — period 2

Al 13 Aluminium 27 | Si 14 Silicon 28 | P 15 Phosphorus 31 | S 16 Sulphur 32 | Cl 17 Chlorine 35 | Ar 18 Argon 40 — period 3

Fe 26 Iron 56 | Co 27 Cobalt 59 | Ni 28 Nickel 59 | Cu 29 Copper 64 | Zn 30 Zinc 65 | Ga 31 Gallium 70 | Ge 32 Germanium 73 | As 33 Arsenic 75 | Se 34 Selenium 79 | Br 35 Bromine 80 | Kr 36 Krypton 84 — period 4

Ru 44 Ruthenium 101 | Rh 45 Rhodium 103 | Pd 46 Palladium 106 | Ag 47 Silver 108 | Cd 48 Cadmium 112 | In 49 Indium 115 | Sn 50 Tin 119 | Sb 51 Antimony 122 | Te 52 Tellurium 128 | I 53 Iodine 127 | Xe 54 Xenon 131 — period 5

Os 76 Osmium 190 | Ir 77 Iridium 192 | Pt 78 Platinum 195 | Au 79 Gold 197 | Hg 80 Mercury 201 | Tl 81 Thallium 204 | Pb 82 Lead 207 | Bi 83 Bismuth 209 | Po 84 Polonium 210 | At 85 Astatine 210 | Rn 86 Radon 222 — period 6

Hs 108 Hassium 265 | Mt 109 Meitnerium 266

Dy 66 Dysprosium 163 | Ho 67 Holmium 165 | Er 68 Erbium 167 | Tm 69 Thulium 169 | Yb 70 Ytterbium 173 | Lu 71 Lutetium 175

Cf 98 Californium 250 | Es 99 Einsteinium 254 | Fm 100 Fermium 257 | Md 101 Mendelevium 258 | No 102 Nobelium 259 | Lr 103 Lawrencium 262

In a pure element such as carbon, all atoms are exactly the same. Yet carbon has different features depending on how the atoms are joined – from black crumbly coal, and the graphite of a pencil, to shiny, clear, ultra-hard diamond.

Atoms are 'friendly'. It's very rare for them to exist on their own. Usually they are joined to many other atoms, in their billions and trillions, to make up the objects and materials around us.

An oxygen molecule

MOLECULES

When an atom joins to one or more other atoms, it forms a molecule. Countless examples are floating around us all the time – oxygen. This gas makes up one-fifth of air and we must breathe it to stay alive. Each molecule of oxygen is made of two oxygen atoms linked or bonded together, and written as the formula O_2.

Pure oxygen is used by rockets, to burn their fuel in space where there is no oxygen.

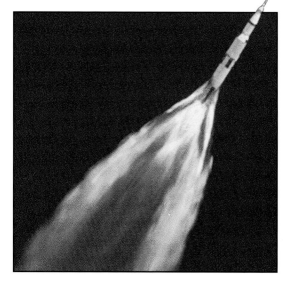

Old-time airships floated because they contained vast numbers of the smallest, lightest atoms – hydrogen. These usually join in pairs, H_2, to form hydrogen gas, which is much lighter than the mixture of gases in air.

COMPOUNDS

Oxygen gas is a pure element because it contains only oxygen atoms. When an atom joins to one or more atoms of different chemical elements, it forms a molecule of a substance known as a compound. We must drink one of the most familiar compounds every day to stay alive – water. Each molecule of water is made of one oxygen atom linked or bonded to two hydrogen atoms. It is written as H_2O.

A water molecule has a V-like shape with one oxygen atom joined to two hydrogens, which are much smaller. Molecules like this are unimaginably tiny. One drop of water contains 100 billion billion molecules.

BREAKING WATER

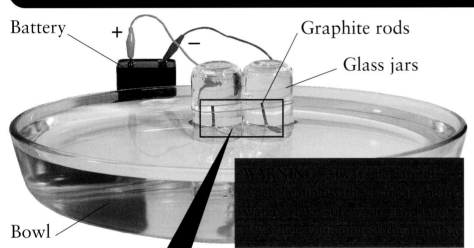

Battery
+
−
Graphite rods

Glass jars

Bowl

Bubbles of pure oxygen

Bubbles of pure hydrogen

WARNING: Always be careful when dealing with electricity and water. Make sure your hands are dry when you connect the battery.

Water is hydrogen and oxygen. These are gases that become liquid when they form water. Electrolysis is using electricity to cause chemical changes.

Electricity can be used to break up water molecules. Put graphite rods, such as those found inside pencils, in a bowl of water and vinegar. Put a jar over each rod, with room for the water to flow beneath. Connect the rods to a 9-volt battery and look for bubbles.

How it WORKS

1 The rods carry electricity down into the water, where two hydrogen atoms are linked, or bonded, to each oxygen atom.

2 The electricity in the water between the rods is enough to break the bonds in each water molecule.

3 Oxygen bubbles collect on the rod connected to the positive battery terminal (the anode). Hydrogen bubbles collect on the rod connected to the negative battery terminal (the cathode).

A car scrap yard or rubbish tip is full of change. Chemical substances come together and alter or react with each other to produce different substances and one example is rust.

VERY SLOW

Rust is a chemical substance formed when iron (the metal which makes up most of steel) reacts with oxygen in the air. The result is a reddish-brown flaky powder called ferric oxide, Fe_2O_3 or rust. (Fe is the chemical formula for iron, which was once called ferrum.) This is an example of a chemical reaction. However it happens very slowly, and it needs dampness to help it along. Iron and steel left in very dry places hardly rust at all.

In a chemical reaction, the starting substances are called reactants. In this example they are iron in the plate and oxygen in the air. The end result is known as the product, and here it is rust.

WARNING – ERUPTION!

Volcanos erupt when red-hot rock spurts through Earth's outer layer. This smaller version involves a chemical reaction.

Pour two tablespoons of baking powder into a small plastic bottle. Put this on a tray to protect your table and build a papier-mâché 'volcano' around it. Add a few drops of food colouring to a tablespoon of vinegar, then pour it into the bottle. It carries out a chemical reaction with the baking powder, fizzes, and sends red 'rock' bubbling out of the volcano.

VERY FAST

A much faster chemical reaction is burning or combustion, such as a candle flame. Again this needs oxygen in the air. The waxy substances in the candle break apart with heat and join or combine with oxygen. The results are energy as light and heat, which are the flame, plus various gases and particles, as smoke. Once started, the reaction continues using its own heat.

Many chemical changes, such as rusting, happen faster in warmer conditions. But some, for example burning, do not start until the temperature rises above a certain level. This is why a candle must be lit with a flame.

How it WORKS

Baking powder contains a chemical substance known as sodium bicarbonate (sodium hydrogencarbonate, $NaHCO_3$). Vinegar contains a substance called ethanoic (acetic) acid (CH_3COOH). When the two come together they react and give off a gas, carbon dioxide. This forms bubbles and makes the volcano 'erupt'.

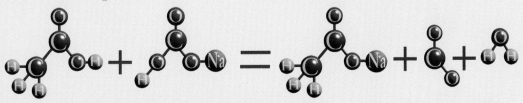

Acetic acid	+	Sodium bicarbonate	=	Sodium acetate	+	Carbon dioxide	+	Water
CH_3COOH		$NaHCO_3$		CH_3COONa		CO_2		H_2O

The bubbling of a chemical reaction can be used to make foam plastics, including sponges and expanded polystyrene sheets for insulation. A foaming chemical is added to the plastic mix, which is then put into a mould where it sets.

Most of the time, when objects and substances are added together, they do not take part in chemical reactions. But they may get totally mixed up, and it can be tricky to separate them.

PHYSICAL, NOT CHEMICAL

A mixture is a combination of substances or materials which have not undergone chemical reactions to form new products. The substances can become very mixed, especially if they are liquids or small particles like powders. Sometimes the substances have to be separated when, for example, an oil spill mixes into sea water. This is done by physical means rather than chemical methods.

Substances like paints, inks and textile dyes are often mixtures of several different colours, or pigments.

To separate gold from sand, prospectors swill them around in a pan with water. Gold is denser than sand and so it is left in the bottom of the pan.

HIDDEN COLOURS

You can split the different pigments used in felt-tip pens using the method known as chromatography, which means 'writing with colours'.

You need various dark felt-tip pens, blotting paper, jars, clips and water. Tear the blotting paper into strips and put a blob of ink on one end of each. Put a small amount of water in each jar and clip the strips to the jars with their ends just reaching the water. Watch and wait. The water creeps up the paper, leaving a trail of colours!

As the water soaks up through each colouring, it carries the mixture of pigments, either dissolved or as tiny particles. Since the pigments have various different sizes and shapes of molecules, they travel at different speeds through the paper and become separate, leaving a trail.

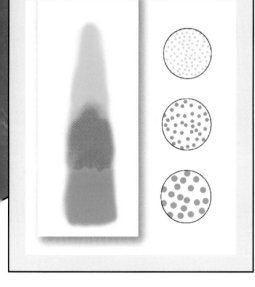

SEPARATE AGAIN

There are several physical ways of separating a mixture's substances, or constituents. One is temperature, when one constituent is frozen into a solid or heated until it becomes a gas, while the other is not. Another is dissolving, for example, when water is added to salt and sand, only the salt dissolves. Or filters can be used, with holes that catch larger particles, and let smaller ones pass through.

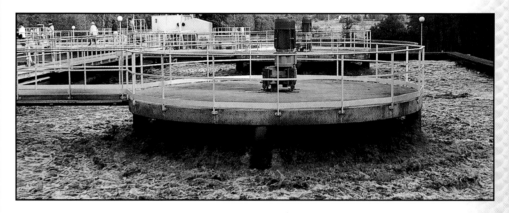

In waste water treatment, net-like screens are used to filter out solids. The holes reduce in size with each screen, to trap smaller objects or particulates, and leave only liquid water.

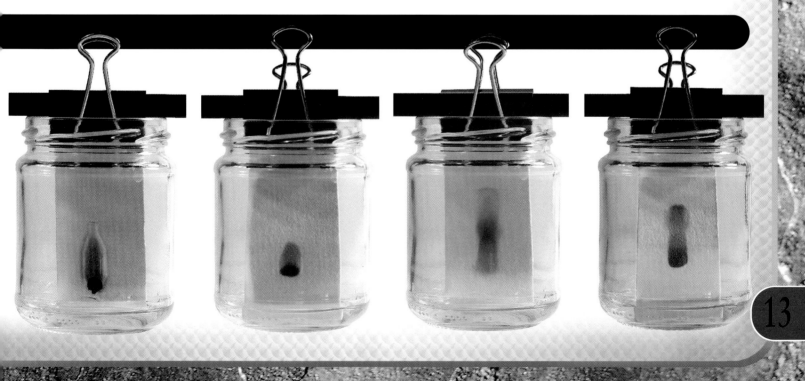

Most of the objects and chemical substances around us, like woods, plastics, bricks and metals, are solids. They hold or retain their shape, unlike liquids and gases (see next pages).

HARDNESS AND BRITTLENESS

Solids vary greatly in their features, such as hardness and brittleness. Metals such as steel are hard, while some plastics are very soft. An iron rod could bend into a U shape, but one of ceramic material would snap because it is brittle. Some solids, such as metals and jewels, are shiny or sparkling. Others look dull, no matter how much they are polished.

One of the rarest solids is gold. It is shiny, it is ductile (can be shaped into many designs), and it lasts for thousands of years.

If you held a cork in one hand, and a same-sized piece of stone in the other, the stone would feel heavier because it is denser. Density is a feature of any substance, solid or liquid or gas.

Chalk is a very light, powdery and brittle solid. The main compound in chalk is calcium carbonate, $CaCO_3$.

How it **WORKS**

When an object is put into water, the water pushes up on it with a force known as upthrust, and helps to support it. If this upthrust is more than the object's weight, the object floats. If the upthrust is less, the object sinks. The amount of upthrust is the same as the weight of the water which the object pushes aside, or displaces. So, floating objects have to be designed to displace water effectively. This is called Archimedes's principle.

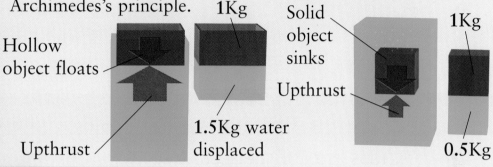

Hollow object floats

1Kg

1.5Kg water displaced

Upthrust

Solid object sinks

Upthrust

1Kg

0.5Kg

Most ships are made of the very strong, long-lasting metal called steel. A rounded lump of steel would sink in water, but if it is made into a hollow shape that pushes water aside it floats.

YET MORE FEATURES

A few solid substances are see-through or transparent, like glass and clear plastic, but most are not. They are opaque. Some solids, especially metals, carry electricity and heat well – they are good conductors. Others like woods and plastics do the opposite and are insulators. All these features and more, including density, help engineers and designers to select the best solid substance for a certain task.

When manufacturing cars, the properties of each solid used, from plastics to ceramics to metals, have to be considered.

Oh no, the drink has spilled everywhere! Solids keep their shape, but fluids are shapeless. They flow, which means they move and spread out, taking the shape of their container.

COLOUR AND TRANSPARENCY

The two main kinds of fluids are liquids such as water and oil, and gases like air (see next page). All liquids flow, but like solids they vary greatly in other features, such as density, and how they carry heat or electricity. Some liquids are see-through or transparent, like vegetable oil. Others are slightly misty or translucent and yet others are opaque, like tar.

Rock can become liquid lava when it is heated to extreme temperatures deep beneath the Earth's surface. It flows out of a volcano during an eruption.

Like solids, as liquids get warmer they enlarge or expand. In a thermometer, a thin 'thread' of mercury expands up a very narrow tube, to show the temperature. At everyday temperatures, most metals are solid, but mercury is a liquid. It changes or melts from solid to liquid at −38.8°C. For comparison, the metal iron does not melt until it reaches 1535°C.

GO WITH THE FLOW

Colours of liquids also vary, from crude oil (petroleum) which is almost black, to milk which is white and water which is colourless. Water and crude oil differ in another way too. This is the way they flow, called viscosity. Less viscous or 'thin' liquids such as water and vinegar flow easily. More viscous or 'thick' liquids such as syrup and crude oil flow much more slowly.

Knowing how easily a liquid flows – its viscosity – is vital. It affects how fast the liquid will move along pipes.

RESISTING FLOW

You can test a liquid's viscosity with some glasses, marbles, a stopwatch, and some see-through liquids.

Fill the glasses with the liquids below. Drop a marble from the same height into each. Time how long it takes to sink. The liquids in which the marbles sink slowest are the most viscous. Use kitchen scales to weigh the glasses. Are heavier liquids more viscous?

How it WORKS

Viscosity is the resistance of a fluid to flow, either within itself, or to moving past an object or objects moving through it. It is due to 'internal friction', which is the amount of rubbing as the molecules of the liquid move past each other.

Molecules of water

Molecules of honey

Water   Cooking oil   Glycerine   Honey

Gases, like liquids, are fluids. They can flow, move and spread out. However, they do so much more than liquids because a gas expands, or increases its volume, to fill its surroundings.

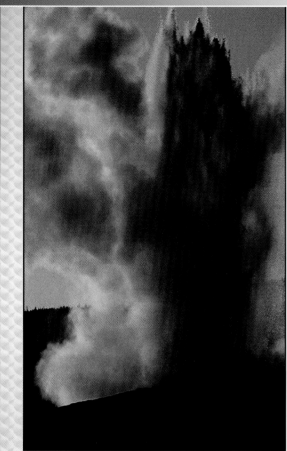

Gas bursts out of a geyser when underground water is heated to boiling point and the steam it creates expands in volume.

SMELLY GASES

Gases have many of the features of liquids, such as colour, transparency, density and viscosity. In general, gases are hundreds of times less viscous than liquids. Another difference is that we taste liquids but we smell gases. The smell of the gas hydrogen sulphide, produced by rotten eggs, makes us wrinkle our noses and cough.

MOVING MOLECULES

Liquids do not change volume easily, but gases do. A liquid's molecules move fairly easily but stay the same distance apart. A gas's molecules move very easily and also change their distance apart. In a sealed container part-filled with liquid, the liquid lies on the bottom. A gas enlarges or expands to fill the whole container.

Nearly all objects become larger or expand when heated, but their mass (weight) stays the same, so they become less dense. The hot air in a balloon is less dense than the cooler air around it, so it floats upwards.

SQUEEZED SMALLER

Changing volume is very useful. Without it, a scuba diver who wanted to stay underwater for an hour would have to take a room-sized tank of air to breathe. However the gases in air can be greatly squeezed or compressed, so their molecules are much closer together, and take up less than one-hundredth of the volume in the scuba tank.

The air in a diver's tank is squeezed, or compressed, over 100 times more than the pressure of ordinary air around us. A device called a regulator reduces this great pressure so the diver can breathe the air normally.

BLOWN UP WITHOUT A PUFF

You can inflate a balloon without blowing or using a pump, by making a gas using a chemical reaction.

Pour a tablespoon of vinegar into a narrow-necked plastic bottle. Then pour two tablespoons of baking powder into a large party balloon. Fit the balloon's neck over the bottle's neck, with the balloon hanging down to keep in the baking powder. Then lift up the balloon. As the substances mix together, they foam and fizz – and the balloon gradually inflates!

Large balloon

Plastic bottle

How it WORKS

The chemical reaction is the same as the one described on page 10. The baking powder and vinegar react to produce a gas, carbon dioxide. As more of this forms, it fills the bottle and pushes up into the balloon, increasing the pressure to make the balloon slowly expand.

Carbon dioxide gas

19

Coffee grains are a solute that dissolve in water. So water is the solvent. When we drink a cup of coffee, we are enjoying a solution.

Stir some sugar into a glass of clean water, and the sugar grains seem to disappear. A sip shows that the sugar is still there, because the water tastes sweet. Where has the sugar gone?

Solution

Solvent

Solute

DISAPPEARING TRICK

The sugar has dissolved. This means its grains have broken apart in the water into tinier and tinier pieces, until they are single molecules. These are far too small for us to see. The substance which dissolves is called the solute, the substance it dissolves in is the solvent, and the two together are known as the solution.

BURSTS OF COLOUR

Oil and water are solvents, and liquids that dissolve into each other are called miscible. Not all liquids can do this.

Put some water in a glass and pour a similar amount of cooking oil on top. They do not mix. The oil is less dense than the water, so it floats. Add some food colouring. The drops sink in the oil layer. Using a spoon, gently push a drop of colouring below the oil. The drop 'bursts' into wispy shapes as the colour spreads through the water.

How it WORKS

The food colouring is miscible with water, but not with oil. So the drops stay intact and do not mix in the upper layer. As soon as the drop enters the water the food colouring dissolves and spreads, or diffuses, to distribute slowly and evenly through the lower layer.

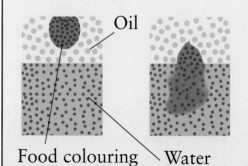

Oil

Food colouring   Water

EXAMPLES OF SOLVENTS

The most familiar solvent is water. Our own bodies are three-fifths water, and thousands of chemical substances dissolved in it take part in the reactions and processes that keep us alive. Salt, sugar, tea and hundreds of *everyday* substances dissolve in it. Less familiar solvents used for dissolving specific substances are nail polish removers, paint-strippers and cleansing products such as drain-cleaners. Industry uses hundreds of powerful solvents including acids, alcohols and ketones, which can be harmful and need careful handling.

Clothes that cannot be washed in a normal machine need to be dry cleaned. Special chemical solvents are used to remove any stains.

Special solvents are sprayed on to an oil spill so it dissolves into tiny pieces, which then spread widely in sea water and do less environmental damage.

What do salt, sugar and rubies have in common? They are all crystals. Each type of crystal has its own shape with flat sides and angled edges, depending on how its molecules fit together.

COMMON CRYSTALS

Crystals are quite common. More than 50 kinds of pure metals exist naturally in crystalline form, but the individual crystals are usually too small to see. They group together into larger lumps which, unlike the crystals, have no definite shape. Metals and other substances combine to form thousands of kinds of minerals which make up rocks and stone, and these are mostly crystals too. Under certain conditions of temperature, pressure and being dissolved deep in the rocks, some minerals slowly form crystals.

Granite is made from igneous rock which cools slowly, leaving big crystals. It is hard-wearing, so it is used for buildings and kerb stones.

Emeralds are crystals of the mineral beryl, tinted green by chromium and vanadium.

How it WORKS

There are about seven different main shapes of crystals, including box-like cubes and triangular pyramids. A crystal's type depends on the shape, size, number and angle of its faces. Here are four simple crystal shapes.

BEAUTIFUL AND USEFUL

Some crystals are made of hard minerals with beautiful colours. They are cut and polished into valuable jewels and gems of various shapes, which are not necessarily the same as the natural crystal. Other crystals have practical uses, like the chemical element silicon, used in the electronics industry.

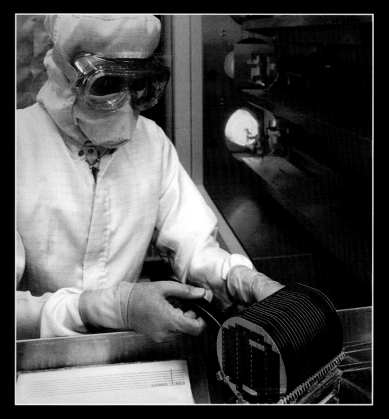

Amethyst is a type of quartz often used in jewellery, although its colour can fade slowly in bright sunlight. It is a hexagonal crystal.

The substance silicon is the second most abundant in the Earth's crust. It is extracted, or purified, from rocks, heated in a furnace and slowly cooled to form long crystals, measuring about one metre, for the electronics industry. Pure crystalline silicon is sliced into very small, thin wafers. Microscopic electronic components are then formed in the surface by using laser light or chemicals to make integrated circuits or 'silicon chips'.

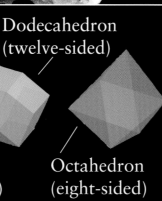

Cube (six-sided)

Dodecahedron (twelve-sided)

Octahedron (eight-sided)

Tetrahedron (four-sided)

These chips are used in a vast array of equipment, especially computers.

This is the warning sign for corrosive chemicals, used to label strong acids and bases.

Two kinds of chemical substances are almost certain to react together. These are acids and bases. If one is added to the other, there may be plenty of fizzing and bubbling, perhaps smoke and fumes – or even an explosion!

Our stomachs can make too much acid for digestion, causing indigestion and heartburn. Taking a substance containing an 'antacid' (base) counteracts it.

OPPOSITES REACT

Acids and bases are 'opposite' kinds of chemicals. Most acids contain the substance hydrogen, such as hydrochloric acid, HCl, and sulphuric acid, H_2SO_4. Most bases are ready to 'steal' this hydrogen, to form a type of chemical substance called a salt. One example is the substance we call 'salt', which is common salt (table or cooking salt). An acid-base reaction, such as that between the acid in vinegar and the base in baking powder, can also make a gas (see page 19).

'Acid rain' contains weak sulphuric acids. Chemicals called sulphates that are found in vehicle exhausts and industrial fumes dissolve in water droplets. When it rains, stone statues can be slowly eaten away.

Many citrus fruits such as lemons and limes contain weak citric acid, which gives them their 'sharp' taste.

HOUSEHOLD USES

Drain-cleaners contain sodium hydroxide or caustic soda, NaOH, which is a strong base that would burn your skin on contact. It is great for cutting through grease and is used in small amounts to make soap. An alkali is a base that dissolves in water.

Green cleaning products use types of acids and bases which are less harmful to the natural environment.

COLOURS FROM CABBAGE

An indicator is a chemical substance that changes colour, depending on whether it mixes with an acid or a base, and how strong this is. You can make your own indicator and show how it works, not in a laboratory but in the kitchen!

Water

Red cabbage

Milk of magnesia

Vinegar

Lemon juice

Paper strips

The indicator strip should turn red for an acid, and blue or green for a base.

Ask an adult to chop a red cabbage into small pieces in a saucepan, cover with water, bring to the boil, simmer gently for 10–15 minutes and allow to cool. (Distilled water, for vehicle batteries, works better than tap water.) Dip small strips of blotting paper into the cabbage water and allow them to dry. Then dip the strips into a household weak acid or base, such as those shown.

How it **WORKS**

The chemical substance from red cabbage is an indicator. When it reacts with an acid it forms a new substance with a red colour. With a base it forms another substance with a blue-green colour. The strength of acids and bases is measured in units called pH. On this scale 1 is the strongest acid, 6 is a weaker acid, 7 is neutral (neither acid nor base), 8 is a weaker base and 14 is the strongest base.

1 2 3 4 5 6 7 8 9 10 11 12 13 14

Strong acid   Pure water   Strong base

25

Most molecules are far too small to see, even with a powerful microscope. But some are giants and a few are so huge they look like specks of dust. They are known as polymers.

BUILDING BRICKS

It may be impossible to see a single house brick from far away, but easy to see the house made from lots of them. In a similar way small 'building brick' molecules known as monomers fit together to build enormous super-molecules called polymers. Many polymers are based on the chemical elements carbon and hydrogen and known as hydrocarbons. If oxygen is added too, they are known as carbohydrates.

Plastics can be hard and stiff. Whether a plastic is hard or bendy depends on the types of monomers it has and how they join to make different polymers.

Some plastics are soft and bendy. They can be used to make plastic bags.

MAKE MILK BENDY

Most plastic is made from petroleum (oil), which formed over millions of years. You can make a plastic-like material using milk. Ask an adult to warm the milk until it simmers. Stir in a few teaspoons of vinegar. Keep stirring and simmering. The milk becomes semi-solid as it cools. Sieve it through a piece of muslin, then squeeze it into a mould.

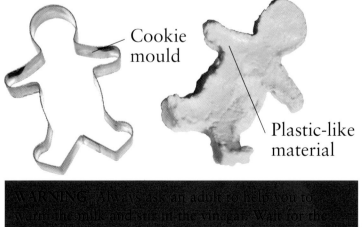

Cookie mould

Plastic-like material

WARNING: Always ask an adult to help you to warm the milk and stir in the vinegar. Wait for the mixture to cool before sieving it.

NATURAL AND ARTIFICIAL

Natural polymers occur in many minerals in rocks, and also in plants and animals and their products, such as cotton, wood and silk. Millions of monomers joined like chains, and millions of chains arranged in bundles, give these fibres flexibility. Artificial versions of these molecular structures are found in glass-fibres, nylons and plastics.

A single fibre of cotton contains billions of molecules of the polymer cellulose, each with over 3500 monomers. These contain carbon, hydrogen and oxygen, the chemical formula $C_6H_{10}O_5$.

Polyethylene (Polymer)   Ethylene (Monomer)

In most polymers, the building-block monomers link end to end like a necklace or chain. This polymer, called polyethylene, is made of thousands of small molecules known as ethylenes or ethenes.

How it WORKS

Small molecules in the milk, including sugar, react with the acidic chemicals in vinegar and polymerize, or join together, to form long chains. These very lengthy macromolecules intertwine and tangle to make the product flexible and squashable.

A racing car's components contain more than 20 special composite materials, for great strength with minimum weight.

COMPOSITES

Polymers are often combined with other substances to make very tough, lightweight materials known as composites. Glass-fibres embedded in a plastic resin form glass-reinforced plastic or GRP, which is both strong and flexible. It has many uses, especially in fast cars and boats.

Iodine < 0.1%
Iron < 0.1%
Magnesium 0.1%
Sodium 0.2%
Chlorine 0.2%
Sulphur 0.3%
Potassium 0.4%
Phosphorus 1.0%

Calcium 1.5%

Nitrogen 3.2%

Hydrogen 9.5%

Carbon 18.5%

Oxygen 65%

If the body could be separated into its smallest parts, the atoms of chemical elements, then oxygen would be top of the list. It forms almost two-thirds of the body's weight, mainly because it is part of water, and the body is three-fifths water.

All objects and materials are made of chemical substances. At its simplest, the human body is a bag of chemicals, which are constantly reacting in the processes of life.

PROTEINS

The chemistry of life is organic, based around the element carbon. The body has several main types of organic molecules. One group is the proteins. At the microscopic level, these form the framework. In skin, the protein keratin gives hard-wearing toughness, while the fibre-like protein collagen adds strength, and elastin allows stretch. Bones contain collagen fibres for slight flexibility, with minerals like calcium phosphate for hardness.

Hair and nails are made almost solely from keratin.

The body develops and maintains itself according to a set of instructions called genes. These are in the form of a chemical, DNA (de-oxyribonucleic acid).

SUGAR AND STARCH

Another huge group of body substances, or biochemicals, is the carbohydrates. Most vital is glucose, also called blood sugar. This high-energy molecule is carried around in the blood to all microscopic cells, where it is broken apart to power living processes.

With the medical condition called diabetes, the level of glucose or blood sugar is not controlled within its usual narrow range. This can cause problems such as fainting and even coma. The level of glucose can be measured by a chemical reaction using a drop of blood.

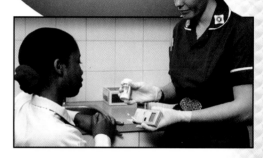

CLOSE CONTROL

The chemicals in our bodies do not interact at random. Many reactions are controlled by substances called enzymes. These are types of protein molecules, each with a special shape. Other molecules fit into the shape, and as they do so, they join together or break apart.

Enzymes speed up or slow down chemical reactions, but they are not altered.

How it **WORKS**

Two vital proteins in muscles are actin and myosin. Each has a long, rope-like shape. Even the smallest muscle has bundles of millions of them. Under the control of enzymes, the actins slide past the myosins and shorten the muscle, so it pulls, moving the body.

Muscle lengthens

Muscle shortens

Actin / Myosin

29

pH SCALE

The 'pH' scale of acidity means 'percentage of hydrogen ion concentration'. Here are some everyday examples:

Car battery acid	2	Soaps	9–10
Lemon juice	3–4	Antacids	11
Acid rain	5–6	Caustic soda	13
	Neutral 7		

THE PERIODIC TABLE

The table or chart of chemical elements shown on pages 6–7 is known as the periodic table. This is because the rows across the table are known as periods. The first version of the table was devised in 1868–69 by Russian chemist Dmitri Mendeleev. He predicted that gaps or 'holes' in this early table indicated further elements to be discovered, and he was right. We are still finding elements today, although all the natural ones are now known. The newest examples are made artificially by scientific equipment.

ATOMIC NUMBER

This is the number of protons in the nucleus of one atom of an element. It usually equals the number of electrons. Protons have a positive electrical charge and electrons have a negative charge, so equal numbers of them balance out, and the atom as a whole has no charge.

ATOMIC MASS

The atomic mass of an atom is higher than the atomic number because it includes neutrons as well as protons. (The electrons are far tinier and do not add much to the mass of the whole atom.)

ATOMIC STRUCTURE

Protons and neutrons form the nucleus in the centre of an atom. Just as the planets go round the Sun in the solar system, electrons are arranged around the nucleus in shells. The shells and atoms increase in size the further they are from the centre. The smallest shell can hold up to two electrons:

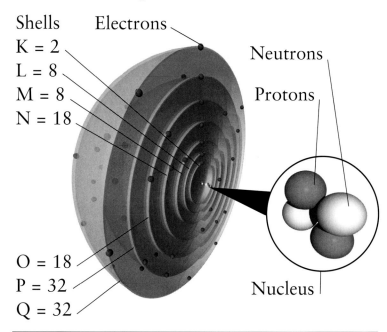

Shells   Electrons

K = 2
L = 8
M = 8
N = 18

O = 18
P = 32
Q = 32

Neutrons

Protons

Nucleus

HOW SMALL ARE ATOMS?

A small atom like one from the very light element lithium measures about 0.3 nanometres across. That means five million atoms in a row would stretch across the dot on this i.

Inside an atom is mostly empty space, since the subatomic particles are even tinier. Imagine the whole atom as a huge sports stadium. The entire nucleus would be the size of a golf-ball in the middle. And the electrons which go around it, right out to the farthest seats, would be smaller than grains of salt.

GLOSSARY

acid

A substance that usually contains hydrogen. When it reacts with a base it loses its hydrogen to form salt and water.

atom

The smallest particle of an element, made up of a central nucleus surrounded by electrons.

base

A substance that can receive hydrogen in a chemical reaction, usually from an acid, to form a salt. The 'opposite' of an acid.

composite

A structural or engineering material which is made from various substances or ingredients, in order to use the most desirable features of each.

compound

A substance made of two or more different elements that are joined together by chemical bonds.

element

A simple or pure substance, containing just one type of atom.

fluid

A substance which can spread out and flow, including liquids and gases.

molecule

Two or more atoms linked or bonded together.

polymer

A large chain-shaped molecule made from many linked repeating subunits (or monomers).

solution

Liquid made when a substance (the solute) dissolves in a liquid (the solvent).

viscosity

A measure of how easily a fluid flows, from very easily in 'thin' liquids like water, to hardly at all in 'thick' liquids like tar.